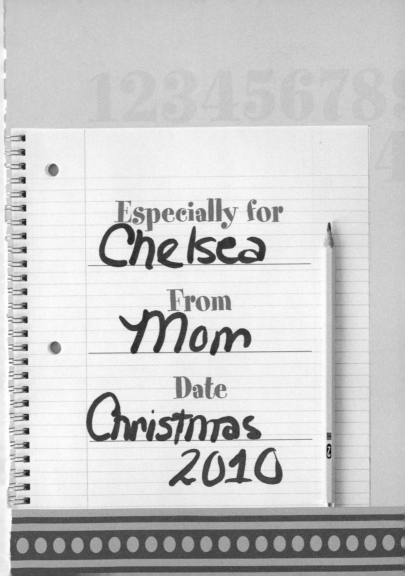

Especially for
Chelsea

From
Mom

Date
**Christmas
2010**

Time-Out
for Teachers

BARBOUR
PUBLISHING

Day
1

Why God Made Teachers

God understood our thirst for knowledge
and our need to be led by someone wiser;
He needed a heart of compassion,
of encouragement and patience. . .someone
who could see potential and believe in the
best in others, so He made teachers.

—UNKNOWN

Serving Others

The term *servant* seems so lowly. However, Christ came and showed us that it is through serving others that we receive life. Being Christ's servant is a high honor given to those who follow Him wholeheartedly.

Daily Prayers

Remind me as I walk the halls
of this school to pray for the
students who pass through them.
Help my teaching to affect many
students for the good. Amen.

Learning to Teach

Lord, help me to strive to give my all to the students who are so eager to learn. Help me to teach them successful strategies while they are still so willing to try. Let me never squelch a desire to learn.

—PAMELA KAYE TRACY

Trust in the Future

Father, teach me to trust that You know
what's best for me and that You are holding
me in the palm of Your hand. Thank You for
the peace that passes all understanding—the
peace that knows my future is safe with You.
Amen.

Day 6

Leadership

If you have leaders who do not recognize God's call on their lives, don't give up. Pray regularly that He will touch their hard hearts. . . . God may make surprising alterations.

Blessings

Our real blessings often appear
to us in the shape of pains, losses,
and disappointments; but let us
have patience and we soon shall
see them in their proper figures.

—JOSEPH ADDISON

Day 8

No Compass Necessary

Teach me, Lord, to rely on You rather than my own understanding. I trust You totally. You are the only map I need if I will just be patient and wait for Your direction. Amen.

Day
9

Humility + Honesty = Bravery

Humility often requires courage.
We assume people will think poorly of us
if we admit we don't know all the facts.
But often just the opposite is true.
Be honest and roll up your sleeves to learn.

Life's Riches

Lord Jesus, as I remember all of Your benefits, I cannot help but praise You and bless Your name. My home, my health, my job, my students: such abundant riches! Truly I have much to be thankful for. I recognize that it all comes from Your hand.

—DENISE SHUMWAY

Finding What
Is Lost

Aren't you excited when you find a
piece of paperwork that has been
lost? Jesus finds joy when one
lost soul comes into the kingdom.
He awaits each one to come and
accept Him as Lord and Savior.

**Day
12**

Play School

You must train the children to their studies in a playful manner and without any air of constraint with the further object of discerning more readily the natural bent of their respective characters.

—PLATO

Day
13

What Really Matters

Help me, Lord, to avoid wasting time and
energy on the things that don't really matter
and to concentrate on the things that will
make a difference in students' lives. Amen.

Day
14

Life Is a Torch

Life is no brief candle to me.
It is a sort of splendid torch
which I have got ahold of for
the moment, and I want to
make it burn as brightly as
possible before handing it on
to future generations.

—GEORGE BERNARD SHAW

Influence

The true teacher defends his
pupils against his own personal
influence. He inspires
self-distrust. He guides their
eyes from himself to the spirit
that quickens him. He will
have no disciple.

—AMOS BRONSON ALCOTT

Day 16

Personal Inventory

Sometimes no matter how hard you work or how large your paycheck is, it's difficult to make ends meet. Take an inventory of your life: Are you in right standing with God? Is your spending out of control? Are you following your budget? God will bless an obedient heart.

Day
17

Spreading Joy

Father, I thank You that You surround me
with children. I spend much of my workday
listening to laughter, seeing smiles,
and getting hugs. How You've blessed me.
Help me, Father, to spread this environment
to the rest of the world.

—PAMELA KAYE TRACY

Day 18

Second Chances

Lord, give me the courage to try again, even though I know I am probably not finished with failing. Thank You for being the God of second chances. Amen.

Leaving the
Past Behind

Are you mourning over
something God has asked
you to leave behind—a failed
relationship, a financial loss,
or a work-related change?
Trust in God that what He asks
you to leave, He will replace with
something infinitely better.

Day 20

Little Children

"Let the little children come to me, and do not hinder them, for the kingdom of God belongs to such as these. I tell you the truth, anyone who will not receive the kingdom of God like a little child will never enter it."

—MARK 10:14–15 NIV

Each Student Is Different

Lord, give me patience to deal with the bright
child who doesn't learn or work the same
as the other children. Help me to adjust my
teaching methods to each student's need.
Amen.

Day
22

Plan Ahead

Schedules tend to become full
to overflowing. Set aside
a portion of your day for
planning. Be realistic when you
set your to-do list and goals.
Rome wasn't built in a day.

Don't Sweat the Small Stuff

Instead of focusing on differences of opinion, Lord, help me look to You, my perfect Brother. Then the small things my Christian brothers and sisters do will not make me stumble, and the large issues will be settled. Amen.

Day 24

Unconditional Love

God accepts you right where you are in life. He has called you to love others regardless of their social status. Keep your arms open wide to show His love.

The Power of One

I am only one, but I am still one; I cannot do
everything, but I can still do something;
and because I cannot do everything, I will
not refuse to do the something that I can do.

—EDWARD EVERETT HALE

Day 26

A Generous Heart

It's amazing what you receive in return when you freely give encouragement and support to others. Giving needs to be done from a generous heart that's thankful for God's blessings.

Finding Solutions

Lord Jesus, keep our eyes open
to the needs around us.
Whether it's a student who needs
shoes, a teacher who needs a
break, or a parent who needs help
learning to read, may we see and
be involved in finding solutions.

—DENISE SHUMWAY

**Day
28**

Humble Life

Whenever I feel pressure to exalt myself above others, Lord, remind me that my worth is found in You alone. Teach me to serve, to love, to be honest, to put the needs of others first—to live a humble but blessed life. Amen.

Day 29

Today's a New Day

Lord, remind me to embrace each new
morning, determined that it will be my finest
day of teaching yet, and to greet my students
as if this will be the best day of their lives.
Amen.

Grading Scale

If I ran a school. . .I'd give the
top grades to those who made
a lot of mistakes and told me
about them, and then told me
what they learned from them.

—R. Buckminster Fuller

A Winning Method

The task of the excellent teacher is to stimulate "apparently ordinary" people to unusual effort. The tough problem is not in identifying winners; it is in making winners out of ordinary people.

—K. PATRICIA CROSS

Day 32

Waking Up to God's Word

Instead of listening to the radio when you first wake up, take time to meditate on God's Word. This will prepare your heart and mind for all He has for you.

Day
33

Life's Lesson

Teach me, Lord, to bring to everyone all that I
am and all that I do as a consciousness of You.
May I be known as a Christian first and
a teacher second. Amen.

Higher Education

You are here in order to enable the world to live more amply, with greater vision, with a finer spirit of hope and achievement. You are here to enrich the world, and you impoverish yourself if you forget the errand.

—WOODROW WILSON

Teaching Kindness

We think of the effective teachers we have had over the years with a sense of recognition, but those who have touched our humanity we remember with a deep sense of gratitude.

—ANONYMOUS

Day 36

Add God to the Equation

Are you doing good works that will last for eternity, or will what you mean for good turn to sand because you lack a relationship with God? Lasting good occurs only when God is in the equation.

Day
37

Classroom Change

Being "completely humble and gentle"
is exactly what I need to make a difference
in my classroom, Lord. Change me so that
others will see You in my life.

—DENISE SHUMWAY

Day 38

God's Gift

God sends us children. . .to enlarge our hearts, to make us unselfish and full of kindly sympathies and affections, to give our souls higher aims, to call out all our faculties to extended enterprise and exertion; to bring round our fireside bright faces and happy smiles, and loving, tender hearts.

—MARY HOWITT

Day
39

Nurturing Hand

Help me to find time to give
attention to the slow child—
to nurture his learning. Help me
to teach at his pace and never
to drive him to frustration. Amen.

Day 40

Diligence

Be diligent in these matters; give yourself wholly to them, so that everyone may see your progress. Watch your life and doctrine closely. Persevere in them, because if you do, you will save both yourself and your hearers.

—1 TIMOTHY 4:15-16 NIV

Day
41

Words of Encouragement

Flatter me, and I may not believe you.
Criticize me, and I may not like you.
Ignore me, and I may not forgive you.
Encourage me, and I may not forget you.

—WILLIAM ARTHUR WARD

Day 42

The Value of Honesty

Everyone makes mistakes on the job, but not everyone is willing to admit them. Being honest may cause you extra work in the short run, but in the long run, you will gain respect from your boss and coworkers.

Leading Future Leaders

In our classroom "kingdoms" where we rule and reign each day, may we be righteous leaders. We want to bring You blessing as we set an example of effective leadership for our students. May they see Your character in our actions and reactions as we lead.

—DENISE SHUMWAY

**Day
44**

More Than a Job

Are you content with your job? Does it pay
you enough to live on? Do you enjoy the
work? Then don't give it up for a job that pays
better but won't bring you much satisfaction—
especially if it puts you at odds with God.

Bearing the Truth

It is so hard to be the bearer of unwanted news. Help me, Lord, to speak the truth in a manner pleasing to You. Help me look for ways to help the students, the parents, and myself. Stay beside the struggling children and lift them up.

—PAMELA KAYE TRACY

Bed Head

Lord, let me see beyond
rumpled hair and stained
shirts, behind freckles,
inside squirming bodies,
past daydreamy eyes to the
child—to the wonderful, unique
person each student is. Amen.

Teaching Is Learning

We teach what we like to learn and the reason many people go into teaching is vicariously to reexperience the primary joy experienced the first time they learned something they loved.

—STEPHEN BROOKFIELD

Day 48

Don't Worry

If you fail God, do you fear that He will give up on you? It's not a worry you need to spend your time considering. God's nature makes Him faithful even when you have forgotten the meaning of that word.

Day
49

The Light of Understanding

My heart is singing for joy this morning.
A miracle has happened! The light of
understanding has shone upon my little pupil's
mind, and behold, all things are changed.

—ANNE SULLIVAN

All Good Deeds Count

Do all the good you can, by all
the means you can, in all the
ways you can, in all the places
you can, at all the times you
can, to all the people you can,
as long as ever you can.

—JOHN WESLEY

Lessons That Last

Inspire me with ideas that will make students' lessons more meaningful to them. Help me to teach so that my students will remember their lessons long after class is dismissed. Amen.

Day 52

School Subject

Upon the subject of education, not presuming to dictate any plan or system respecting it, I can only say that I view it as the most important subject which we as a people may be engaged in.

—ABRAHAM LINCOLN

Day
53

Working Hard

No matter what kind of person you work for, that person is not in control of your future. You depend on God, not the people around you. As you work hard, God will do His part and put you in the position He wants for you.

Priorities

You give richly to Your children.
Everything I need is mine for
the asking, but blessings come
in Your time, not mine.
Help me keep my priorities in
order, Father, trusting that You
will provide what I need, when
I need it, in the way I need it.
Amen.

Flickering Flame

At times our own light goes out
and is rekindled by a spark from
another person. Each of us has
cause to think with deep gratitude
of those who have lighted the
flame within us.

—ALBERT SCHWEITZER

Day 56

Taking Responsibility

It is the responsibility of every adult. . .to make sure that children hear what we have learned from the lessons of life and to hear over and over that we love them and that they are not alone.

—MARIAN WRIGHT EDELMAN

Day 57

Problem Solver

Sometimes it feels like God is far away.
No matter what you're going through,
however, God is right beside you. When you
pray, He is working out problems that you
couldn't begin to solve on your own.

To Learn or Not to Learn

The teachers who get "burned out" are not the ones who are constantly learning, which can be exhilarating, but those who feel they must stay in control and ahead of the students at all times.

—FRANK SMITH

The Tide Will Turn

When you get into a tight place
and everything goes against you,
till it seems as though you could
not hang on a minute longer,
never give up then, for that is just
the place and time that the
tide will turn.

—HARRIET BEECHER STOWE

Day 60

Work with Your Hands

Study to be quiet, and to do your own business, and to work with your own hands, as we commanded you; that ye may walk honestly toward them that are without, and that ye may have lack of nothing.

—1 THESSALONIANS 4:11–12 KJV

Day
61

Mastering Creativity

God is the Master Creator. When you
need creativity for a project, you know
where to turn. He is able to give you insight
and ideas you've never had before.

Day
62

Teachers of All Sizes

Lord, remind me not to rush
through lessons. Remind me to
not only encourage questions,
but to also allow others to give
the answers. Remind me to let
the little children take on the role
of teacher. These precious ones
are often more perceptive than I.

—PAMELA KAYE TRACY

Work of Love

Heavenly Father, You know me
inside and out. You fashioned
me in the way You saw best,
according to Your unique purpose
and plan for my life. Help me
spend more time praising You for
Your work of love. Amen.

**Day
64**

Happy Days

Try to make at least one person happy every day, and then in ten years you may have made three thousand six hundred and fifty persons happy, or brightened a small town by your contribution to the fund of general enjoyment.

—SYDNEY SMITH

Priorities

When you enter your workplace each day,
take a few minutes to prioritize the tasks that
need to be accomplished. Staying focused will
help you walk away from the day with
a feeling of accomplishment.

Day 66

Have Hope!

I know there are many things I cannot control, no matter how hard I may try, and many of life's events break my heart. Still I have hope, because through it all I have You. Thank You, Lord, for hope. Amen.

It's a Wonderful Life

Teach me how to impart the
wonder of life to my students.
Help me to show them that they
are already living their lives,
not preparing to live. Amen.

Day 68

Community Service

Our work is meant to be a grace. It is a blessing and a gift, even a surprise and an act of unconditional love toward the community— and not just the present community. . .but the community to come, the generations that follow our work.

—MATTHEW FOX

Day
69

Faith in the Workplace

Have you ever heard two people describe
the same meeting and wondered how their
perceptions could be so different?
People bring their fears and their faith into
the workplace and see things in light of them.
So do you. Keep that in mind.

Day 70

Getting Satisfaction

Look at a day when you are supremely satisfied at the end. It is not a day when you lounge around doing nothing; it is when you have had everything to do, and you have done it.

—MARGARET THATCHER

Reading Is Power

How many a man has dated a new era in his life from the reading of a book! The book exists for us, perchance, that will explain our miracles and reveal new ones.

—HENRY DAVID THOREAU

Teamwork

When people rejoice with those who are happy and hurt for the sorrowful, they work better together. A team cares about what's on the heart of each member. So care for your team.

Day
73

All Hands Raised

Lord, help me to reach out to the hesitant
students who lack the self-confidence to
speak up in class. Teach me how to bring
them out of their shells. Amen.

Motivation

God is an expert motivator.
Ask Him for ways to motivate
your staff members. Yes,
everyone needs a paycheck, but
don't forget that recognition and
appreciation can go a long way.

The Strength of Cheerfulness

Wondrous is the strength of cheerfulness, and its power of endurance—the cheerful man will do more in the same time, will do it better, will preserve it longer, than the sad or sullen.

—THOMAS CARLYLE

Day 76

Training Days

The great end of education is to discipline rather than to furnish the mind; to train it to the use of its own powers, rather than fill it with the accumulation of others.

—TYRON EDWARDS

Safe Haven

Lord, there are children out there who are
not in loving homes. There are children who
come to school, and it is their only safe haven.
Lord, watch over those children. And give
me the wisdom to know how to help. Let my
frustrations be followed by action.

—PAMELA KAYE TRACY

God on the Job

You're working to please God,
but did you know He has also
been working for you? Every day
when you get up, you can count
on God's protection and guidance
and the work of His Spirit.

Reaching Peak Potential

Let us think of education as the means of developing our greatest abilities, because in each of us there is a private hope and dream which, fulfilled, can be translated into benefit for everyone and greater strength of the nation.

—JOHN F. KENNEDY

Day 80

Giving Is Also Receiving

"Give, and you will receive. Your gift will return to you in full—pressed down, shaken together to make room for more, running over, and poured into your lap. The amount you give will determine the amount you get back."

—LUKE 6:38 NLT

Day
81

Daily Blessings

The sun. . .in its full glory, either at rising or setting—this, and many other like blessings, we enjoy daily. And for most of them, because they are so common, most men forget to pay their praises. But let not us.

—IZAAK WALTON

Golden Rest

Thank You for the peaceful
moments and the rest that come
during evenings, weekends,
and holidays when class is out.
Thank You for time to fellowship
with family. Amen.

Keeping the Faith

When a man works, his wages are not credited to him as a gift, but as an obligation. However, to the man who does not work but trusts God who justifies the wicked, his faith is credited as righteousness.

—ROMANS 4:4–5 NIV

Self-Taught

The pupil can only educate himself. Teachers are the custodians of apparatus upon which he himself must turn and twist to acquire the excellencies that distinguish the better from the poorer of God's vessels.

—MARTIN H. FISCHER

Difficult Tests

Lord Jesus, like my students, I am being
tested. But my tests are through trials—
many kinds of trials. Help me to have this
view in difficulties: You are testing my faith
for a reason—to develop perseverance
so that I can be mature.

—Denise Shumway

From Generation to Generation

Bear in mind that the wonderful things you learn in your schools are the work of many generations. All this is put into your hands as your inheritance in order that you may receive it, honor it, add to it, and one day faithfully hand it on to your children.

—ALBERT EINSTEIN

Home, Sweet Home

Godly relationships can strengthen your work life. If you have love and support at home, it can give you a boost to do all you are called to do at work.

Day 88

Facing the World

Father, I'm not strong enough to face the world alone; too much of it is out of my control. I want to be motivated by love. So I'm putting my faith in You. Amen.

Day 89

Seeking Security

When you feel lost and scattered, when life no longer makes sense, turn to Jesus. Ask Him to lead you. No matter what happens to your job, you will have the security of being God's child.

Day
90

True and Noble

Finally, brothers, whatever
is true, whatever is noble,
whatever is right, whatever
is pure, whatever is lovely,
whatever is admirable—
if anything is excellent or
praiseworthy—think
about such things.

—PHILIPPIANS 4:8 NIV

The Eternal Lesson

The world is not a playground;
it is a schoolroom. Life is not a
holiday, but an education.
And the one eternal lesson for us
all is how better we can love.

—HENRY DRUMMOND

Day 92

Maintaining Sanity

Lord, thank You for keeping me sane in middle age. I want neither a tattoo nor a pacifier. Keep me sane a little longer, and help me strive to grow in the knowledge and understanding of You.

—PAMELA KAYE TRACY

Day
93

Important Labor

God has given you your abilities, put you in your workplace, and placed His Spirit in your heart. When you serve others, no matter what your job title or pay scale, you are doing the most important labor of all—God's work.

Praying throughout the Day

Lord Jesus, I want to be faithful in praying for those I work with and for our class as we work together with our students. Help me to turn to You many times during the day, bringing each situation to You.

—DENISE SHUMWAY

Dear Children

I realize, Lord, that You had
more to do with the flowering of
my children than I did. I did the
best I could, and You magnified
my efforts. Thank You for all the
effort You put into my children.
May You rejoice in them as
much as I do. Amen.

Day 96

Beautiful Aspirations

Far away there in the sunshine are my highest aspirations. I may not reach them, but I can look up and see their beauty, believe in them, and try to follow where they lead.

—LOUISA MAY ALCOTT

Day
97

Good Choice

One poor choice can become a stumbling
block in a career. Imagine what a series of
poor choices can do. God will give you His
wisdom—all you have to do is ask.

Classroom Handiwork

Oh God, bless the work of my hands. May I make a difference in the life of every young person who comes through the door of my classroom. Amen.

Natural Gift

Teaching is the only major
occupation of man for which we
have not yet developed tools that
make an average person capable
of competence and performance.
In teaching we rely on the
"naturals," the ones who somehow
know how to teach.

—PETER DRUCKER

Day 100

Love Wisdom

Don't turn your back on wisdom, for she will protect you. Love her, and she will guard you. Getting wisdom is the wisest thing you can do! And whatever else you do, develop good judgment.

—PROVERBS 4:6–7 NLT

Day
101

Constructive Criticism

Whenever constructive criticism comes to
you on the job, take it seriously and evaluate
where you can improve. Iron does sharpen
iron, and God will allow people to speak truth
to you in order for you to grow.

Childish Responses

Heavenly Father, like a child,
I do not always welcome
correction. I pout; I avoid You;
I try to go my own way. In times
like those, please be patient
with me. Amen.

Day 103

Leading with a Sharp Stick

The dream begins with a teacher who believes in you, who tugs and pushes and leads you to the next plateau, sometimes poking you with a sharp stick called "truth."

—DAN RATHER

Day 104

Organization

Take time to organize your workspace so you can increase your efficiency. If you are not good at organizing, ask a coworker who has a strength in this area.

An Open Door

When one door closes, another one opens,
but we often look so long and regretfully
at the closed door that we fail to see
the one that has opened for us.

—ALEXANDER GRAHAM BELL

Make Learning Contagious

Once children learn how to learn, nothing is going to narrow their mind. The essence of teaching is to make learning contagious, to have one idea spark another.

—Marva Collins

A New Job

Things always look promising
at the beginning of a new job.
To keep it that way, you will need
to make good choices. Ask the
Lord to guide you daily.

Day 108

Dealing with Disappointment

Father, help me to keep a cheerful outlook when a student disappoints me. When a student refuses to try to learn, give me ideas to help motivate him. Amen.

Day 109

Choose Your Words

No doubt you've had it happen—you try to say the right thing, but awful words trip off your tongue. Out of the abundance of the mouth the heart speaks. Be sure to clear up minor concerns before they become major ones and come spilling out.

Day
110

Comfort

Mighty Lord in heaven, grief overwhelms me. I feel alone, even in the midst of friends and family who have come to comfort me. Thank You for the comfort only You can give. Amen.

A Good Teacher

No man can be a good teacher
unless he has feelings of warm
affection toward his pupils and
a genuine desire to impart to
them what he himself believes
to be of value.

—BERTRAND RUSSELL

An Open Heart

Your heart is beating with God's love; open it to others. He has entrusted you with gifts and talents; use them for His service. He goes before you each step of the way; walk in faith. Take courage. Step out into the unknown with the One who knows all.

—ELLYN SANNA

**Day
113**

Learners and Teachers

Learning is finding out what we already know.
Doing is demonstrating that you know it.
Teaching is reminding others that they know
just as well as you. You are all learners,
doers, and teachers.

—RICHARD BACH

Day 114

Goals

Though you may never list them on a piece of paper, you have career goals. Goals help keep you focused and remind you of a future. Ask God to guide you at work and home to make goals count for eternity.

Contributing to Others' Needs

If [a man's gift] is encouraging,
let him encourage, if it is
contributing to the needs of
others, let him give generously;
if it is leadership, let him govern
diligently; if it is showing mercy,
let him do it cheerfully.

—ROMANS 12:8 NIV

**Day
116**

Voice of Reason

Father, let me be a voice of reason, able to
articulate my position calmly and clearly.
When I need to admit that I'm wrong,
give me Your courage to do so. Amen.

Success on the Job

It's easy to become discouraged on the job—
frustrating assignments, difficult people,
unjust situations, missed opportunities.
God has brought you this far, and He'll never
let you down. Trust Him for your success—
today and every day.

Day 118

This World. . .

This world, after all our science
and sciences, is still a miracle:
wonderful, inscrutable,
magical, and more.

—THOMAS CARLYLE

**Day
119**

Listening Skills

It is frustrating, Father, to try to
teach children who have short
attention spans. They seem to
be unable to pay attention.
Help me to teach them listening
skills. Amen.

**Day
120**

Forgiveness

So, as those who have been chosen of
God, holy and beloved, put on a heart of
compassion, kindness, humility, gentleness
and patience; bearing with one another, and
forgiving each other, whoever has a complaint
against anyone; just as the Lord forgave you,
so also should you.

—COLOSSIANS 3:12–13 NASB

Day
121

Reaching Out

Lord, help me to take the time to reach out
and know the words to say to these students
who silently call out for help. I feel so
unprepared for the task, but I know it's what
You would do and what You want me to do.

—PAMELA KAYE TRACY

Day
122

Deadlines

When you feel overwhelmed
with the load at work, take time
to evaluate and ask God for
direction. You may be able to
get assistance from coworkers
or move deadlines. God will
smooth your path and help you
make the most of your time.

Caring for Children

Father of all, You have entrusted
these children to my care, and I
love them without reservation,
just as You love me. May I serve
as an example of Your patience
and undying love when I must
correct them. Amen.

Day 124

Meetings

In meetings, answer responsibly with the facts and leave out your own opinion unless it is asked for. Of course, this may mean taking extra time before the meeting to prepare, but in the long run you will gain the respect of your coworkers.

**Day
125**

Striving to Serve

To desire and strive to be of some service
to the world, to aim at doing something
which shall really increase the happiness
and welfare and virtue of mankind—this is
a choice which is possible for all of us;
and surely it is a good haven to sail for.

—HENRY VAN DYKE

Stepping-Stones

Teachers who inspire realize there will always be rocks in the road ahead of us. They will be stumbling blocks or stepping-stones; it all depends on how we use them.

—UNKNOWN

Walk in Love

Frequently, there is one person
who's impossible to get along with
in the work environment.
God asks you to walk in love
toward all. Do your best to be kind
and honest to everyone.

Day 128

Life and Peace

Lord Jesus, as I give You control over who I am, I can experience life and peace. How I need that in the daily whirl of teaching! Keep me close to You in prayer, and help me set my mind on You alone.

—DENISE SHUMWAY

Day 129

Classroom Dangers

Lord, calm my fear of facing a situation
of grave danger in my classroom. I put my
faith in You. Thank You for promising
to be with me always. Amen.

Righting Wrongs

There are two great injustices that can befall a child. One is to punish him for something he didn't do. The other is to let him get away with doing something he knows is wrong.

—Robert Gardner

The Waiting Game

Time can drag when you are
looking for a new job. God doesn't
promise that it will happen
overnight. The waiting may be part
of what God is doing in your life.
Continue to trust in Him to open
the right door at the right time.

Day 132

Childhood

Lord, let us enjoy our childhood and let maturity unfold naturally. Let us not be so impatient for the passing of time. Let us cherish the now for what it is.

—PAMELA KAYE TRACY

Day 133

Divine Joy

Only when my life is anchored in Your love will my joy endure regardless of the circumstances. And that's the kind of joy I want—steady and enduring. Thank You, Lord, for a heart full of divine joy. Amen.

Day 134

Lessons Learned

God allows us to experience the low points of life in order to teach us lessons we could not learn in any other way. The way we learn those lessons is not to deny the feelings but to find the meanings underlying them.

—STANLEY LINDQUIST

Day
135

Working for God's Glory

Your work makes a difference in people's lives. How you carry out your job is important not only to your boss but to God. Do your work for God's glory, not just the reward of a paycheck.

Day
136

Little Conveniences

Happiness consists more in small conveniences or pleasures that occur every day than in great pieces of good fortune that happen but seldom to a man in the course of his life.

—Benjamin Franklin

Day 137

Be Studious

Get over the idea that only children should spend their time in study. Be a student so long as you still have something to learn, and this will mean all your life.

—HENRY L. DOHERTY

The Pursuit of Excellence

Father, I want to pursue excellence in every area of my life—even though I know that pursuing excellence does not always mean I'll achieve it. Keep me humble and hopeful, clearly dependent on You. Amen.

Voice Your Appreciation

Can you think of those who have had a powerful impact on your career—a trainer, mentor, educator, or boss? Drop that person an e-mail or call and voice your appreciation.

As God Intends

I say, through the grace given unto me,
to every man that is among you, not to think
of himself more highly than he ought to think;
but to think soberly, according as God hath
dealt to every man the measure of faith.

—ROMANS 12:3 KJV

The Home Team

The way a team plays as a whole
determines its success. You may have
the greatest bunch of individual stars in
the world, but if they don't play together,
the club won't be worth a dime.

—BABE RUTH

Day 142

Gaining Knowledge

Lord, keep me stable and
help me strive to grow in my
knowledge and understanding
of You so that I might be blessed
in every part of my teaching
work. Amen.

**Day
143**

A Life's Work

What are you building with your
life? A career or God's kingdom?
You can seek to become important
to other people, or you can seek
to be important to God.

Day 144

A High Hill to Climb

The marvelous richness of human experience would lose something of rewarding joy if there were no limitations to overcome. The hilltop hour would not be half so wonderful if there were no dark valleys to traverse.

—HELEN KELLER

Day
145

A Work to Carry On

Every human being has a work to carry on
within, duties to perform abroad, influence to
exert, which are peculiarly his, and which no
conscience but his own can teach.

—WILLIAM ELLERY CHANNING

Day 146

Problematic Situations

God did not promise a flawless workplace. Instead, He has promised to be there for you when you find yourself in problematic situations. Prayer changes things because God is listening.

Harvest of Blessing

Thank You, Lord, for leading
me to do good things and then
allowing me to reap the harvest of
blessing that follows. You give me
everything I could ever hope for
and will never deserve. Amen.

Big Decisions

Do you worry about decisions your boss, the government, or industry giants make that influence your working life? No matter what choices are made by people in positions of power, no decision is beyond God's intervention.

Day
149

Stop and Listen

Teach me, Father, when to talk and when
to stop and listen. Often a student can work
through the problem herself. Teach me to be
patient and let her try. Amen.

Surpassing the Safe Route

Excellence can be attained if you care more than others think is wise, risk more than others think is safe, dream more than others think is practical, and expect more than others think is possible.

—Unknown

Education Outside of the Classroom

It's so amazing how the lessons of the classroom are demonstrated in adult life. I thank You for these moments that take me back in time and make me smile. I've had so many wonderful years as a teacher. I look forward to many more.

—PAMELA KAYE TRACY

**Day
152**

Assistance

Through your working career, you have probably been helped along the way. Never forget how it made you feel when someone trained you or assisted you when you were overwhelmed. Now it is time to lend a helping hand to others.

Day
153

Constant Prayers

Lord, continue to keep my heart burning to reach those souls who do not know You. May my prayers remain constant, asking that Your Spirit would touch the souls of the unsaved around me. Turn their lives around, Lord, just as You did mine. Amen.

Creating Loving Environments

Lord Jesus, You showed love in Your living and in Your dying. You denied Yourself to obey the Father's plan. May we be channels of this love in our classrooms, in our homes, and in every area of our lives.

—DENISE SHUMWAY

Utilizing Uniqueness

As You have formed every snowflake differently, You have also made each child unique. Teach me to honor that difference and teach the student to turn it to his advantage. Amen.

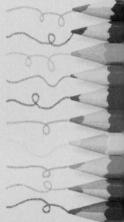

Day 156

Real Success

To appreciate beauty; to find the best in others; to give one's self; to leave the world a little better. . .to know even one life has breathed easier because you have lived. . . . This is to have succeeded.

—RALPH WALDO EMERSON

Day 157

You Can't Buy Happiness

Most people believe that all it would take to keep them happy is a 20 percent raise. Yes, money does help in life, but it will not keep you happy. Only a personal relationship with Jesus Christ will keep you truly fulfilled.

Waiting Patiently

Teach me, Lord, to wait
patiently for Your answers,
Your provisions, Your solutions.
When I am tempted to run off
on my own, restrain me by Your
Spirit. I know my life will be
secure in Your care. Amen.

A Lifetime of Learning

You can teach a student a lesson for a day; but if you can teach him to learn by creating curiosity, he will continue the learning process as long as he lives.

—CLAY P. BEDFORD

Day 160

Seek the Lord

"Sow for yourselves righteousness, reap the fruit of unfailing love, and break up your unplowed ground; for it is time to seek the Lord, until he comes and showers righteousness on you."

—Hosea 10:12 NIV

Day
161

Lead the Way

Lord, show me the potential in every face,
in every pair of hands. Show me where two
little legs may someday walk. May I, as a
teacher, point the way clearly. Amen.

Inspiring Independence

If you would have your children
to walk honorably through the
world, you must not attempt to
clear the stones from their path,
but teach them to walk firmly
over them—not insist upon
leading them by the hand,
but let them learn to go alone.

—ANNE BRONTË

Day 163

Education's True Purpose

The true purpose of education is to cherish and unfold the seed of immortality already sown within us; to develop, to their fullest extent, the capacities of every kind with which the God who made us has endowed to us.

—ANNA JAMES

**Day
164**

Almighty Boss

God is your ultimate boss, and He says you
need to treat your human boss with respect.
At the end of the day, nothing is more
rewarding than imagining our heavenly
Father saying, "Well done."

Day
165

Going Places

Lord, so often You went places where You
weren't wanted. Thank You, Lord,
for choosing not only the safe and welcoming
places. Thank You for reaching out
to hesitant souls.

—PAMELA KAYE TRACY

Day 166

Productivity

I need Your wisdom, Lord.
Help me with my priorities, both
at home and at work. I want to
be productive for Your glory,
but I cannot do it on my own.
Show me where I should change.
Amen.

Don't Give Up

God blots out sin, not because of our character, but because of His. If you are discouraged by your own sinfulness, don't give up—give it to God. He'll forgive your past wrongs and give you strength for new life in Him.

Day 168

A Treasured Feeling

A teacher who can arouse a feeling for one single good action, for one single good poem, accomplishes more than he who fills our memory with rows and rows of natural objects, classified with name and form.

—JOHANN WOLFGANG VON GOETHE

Living with Christian Virtues

Perhaps being small in your own sight isn't such a bad thing. Pride and arrogance are not Christian virtues. Things never go as smoothly when you walk through life without God.

God's Instrument

Lord, make me an
instrument of Thy peace.
Where there is hatred,
let me sow love.
Where there is injury, pardon.
Where there is doubt, faith.
Where there is despair, hope.
Where there is darkness, light.
Where there is sadness, joy.

—FRANCIS OF ASSISI

Long Afternoons

When the afternoon drones on
and my strength wavers, remind
me that You, Lord, are the One
who can transform my weakness
into the strength I need to teach.
Amen.

**Day
172**

Expect Only the Best

God has promised to give you good things if
you obey Him. You may not get the blessing
right now, but don't lose heart; God has not
forgotten you. Be patient and expect only the
best from Him.

Day
173

Accepting Correction

Forgive me when I take Your correction
poorly, Lord. I know that You teach and
correct with love, and little by little I become
the person You want me to be. Amen.

Working Together

Show appreciation to those in your workplace who do low-paying jobs. They may be at the bottom of the workplace pyramid, but they're important to the Lord—and they should be important to you as well.

An Open Mind

How often do I look at a student,
Lord, and misjudge him or her
based on stereotypes? So often,
Lord, You show me the error of
my ways. Lord, help me to make
the choice to keep an open mind
about all Your children.

—PAMELA KAYE TRACY

Day 176

Daily Interactions

Lord Jesus, You are the faithful One. I can trust You to accomplish Your will through me as I interact with my students and other people at school. I believe You called me to be a teacher, even as You called me to salvation.

—Denise Shumway

Day 177

Able Worker

Father God, only You know my talents
and abilities. Call me to the type of service
best suited for me. Forgive my doubts and
fears and show me where I am needed,
that Your will shall be done. Amen.

What Counts

When we start to count flowers,
we cease to count weeds;
When we start to count blessings,
we cease to count needs;
When we start to count laughter,
we cease to count tears;
When we start to count memories,
we cease to count years.

—UNKNOWN

The Circle of Learning

As the school semester unfolds,
Father, show me the students
who need my help the most.
Help me to work to draw them
into the circle of learning. Amen.

**Day
180**

Spreading Comfort
to Others

Blessed be. . .the God of all comfort;
who comforteth us in all our tribulation,
that we may be able to comfort them which
are in any trouble, by the comfort wherewith
we ourselves are comforted of God.

—2 Corinthians 1:3-4 KJV

Good News

You are on a team with God to bring His good news to a hurting world. Every team member is crucial. Whether you are at the beginning of the process or the end, your actions count.

Restful Moments

Father, I know it's important for me to rest, for my sake and for the sake of those who depend on me. Give me wisdom to know which tasks can wait and which can be eliminated so I can get the rest I need. Amen.

Mission Essential

God gave Jonah a mission:
Go to Nineveh to preach.
Though Jonah didn't like the job,
he couldn't quit. If God has given
you a mission you have yet to
fulfill, there is still time to obey.
The rewards of obeying God are
well worth it.

**Day
184**

Marching to a
Different Drum

If a man does not keep pace with his
companions, perhaps it is because he hears
a different drummer. Let him step to the
music which he hears, however measured
or far away.

—HENRY DAVID THOREAU

**Day
185**

The Character of Youth

Thank You, Lord, for showing a doubter like
me that the next generation is not the lost
generation. Make me a strong believer in
the character of youth. Amen.

Obedience Training

Over and over, God tells us to
obey His laws, but nowhere
in scripture does He promise
obedience will be fun—
extremely beneficial, yes, but
not fun. However, the blessings
of following God's law will bring
peace to your life.

Working to the Limit

Only if you reach the boundary
will the boundary recede before
you. And if you don't, if you
confine your efforts, the boundary
will shrink to accommodate itself
to your efforts. And you can
only expand your capacities by
working to the very limit.

—HUGH NIBLEY

Day 188

Worthy Reputation

The reputation that lasts is the one you build carefully, the one that shows what you wholeheartedly believe, the one you act on. Do right consistently; worship God with your whole life and you'll have a reputation worth keeping.

Day
189

Responding to Doubt

Father, when questions arise in my heart,
help me be quick to search Your Word for
the evidence of truth. Keep me daily in the
scriptures so that I will always be ready
to respond to doubt. Amen.

Preparation

I've read Your Word; it contains
math, reading, spelling,
and history in it. It tells of births.
It highlights special days.
And it helps me understand what
heaven will be like. Thank You,
Lord, for preparing me.

—PAMELA KAYE TRACY

Day 191

Unavoidable Interruptions

Work interruptions are inevitable—sickness, car trouble, meetings, emergencies. Once you recognize your need for help on an out-of-control day and trust God to control things, the day will begin to get better.

Day 192

Daily Task

Have courage for the great sorrows of life and patience for the small ones; and when you have laboriously accomplished your daily task, go to sleep in peace. God is awake.

—Victor Hugo

Day
193

Worthy Occupation

Father, when I wonder if what I do is worth
anything, remind me how precious each of
my students is to You and of what an impact a
single day can have in their education. Amen.

Working Together

We desire to be one with You in Your work. May we never wander off to create monuments to ourselves. As we teach, may our lessons and our very lives reflect Your eternal design, turning the hearts of our students to you.

—DENISE SHUMWAY

All You Need Is Love

I know I can't love on my own, Lord, but through Your Spirit I can do all things—even this. When I seek to love others, I need to keep my eyes on You. Sweep away my critical attitude, and fill me with Your love. Amen.

Day 196

Supporting Cast

Don't be afraid to thank supporters.
No matter why they came to your aid,
they were a gift from God. Let them know
that you don't take them for granted.

Day 197

Take Time to Be Kind

Life is short, and we never have enough
time for gladdening the hearts of those who
travel the way with us. Oh, be swift to love!
Make haste to be kind.

—HENRI-FRÉDÉRIC AMIEL

Keen Observation

When the leaves begin to fall, we notice them; but soon there are too many of them, and we no longer notice. Father, may my observation of students never become dull. Keep me enthused and excited about them. Amen.

Without Complaints

When Joseph was thrown into a pit by his brothers, he didn't waste time complaining. Instead, he put his hand to the next job given him and was greatly rewarded. Strive to be a Joseph in your job.

Day 200

Beacons in the Dark

Do all things without grumbling or disputing;
so that you will prove yourselves to be
blameless and innocent, children of God
above reproach in the midst of a crooked
and perverse generation, among whom you
appear as lights in the world.

—PHILIPPIANS 2:14–15 NASB

Day
201

Contentment

Father, help me to remember that it is Your
will for me to be content with my position in
life. As I enter my classroom each morning,
help me to be content. Amen.

Compassion Is Power

Kind words are the music of the world. They have a power which seems to be beyond natural causes, as if they were some angel's song which had lost its way and come on earth.

—Frederick William Faber

Day 203

Aspirations

Dear Jesus, may my life reflect Your transforming work as You renew my mind. Help me show my students that it's okay to be different, when that means being like You. You, Lord—not some popular singer or actor—are the Person we should aspire to be like.

—DENISE SHUMWAY

**Day
204**

Moving beyond Mistakes

Unfortunately, not every work project turns
out well—even if you're committed to the job
and do your best. Don't dwell on it. Learn
what you can from the situation and move on.

Day
205

Unlimited Possibilities

One of the beauties of teaching is that
there is no limit to one's growth as a teacher,
just as there is no knowing beforehand
how much your students can learn.

—Herbert Kohl

The Light of Compassion

No matter what my troubles, Your peace reaches the hurting places within me, Lord. Help me pass comfort on to those who are also in need. Open my heart to Your wisdom and gentleness, and let the light of compassion burn brightly in me. Amen.

Commitment

When a soul enters eternity by
faith in Jesus, all heaven rejoices.
If you've never committed your
life to Jesus Christ, you can
start today. Tell God that you
know you've sinned and need
forgiveness and that you're
trusting in Jesus for that
forgiveness.

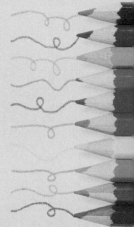

Repairing Wounds

Some days I seem to act more as a nurse and a nanny than an educator, Father. May I bandage scraped knees and pass out tissues with love. Amen.

Day
209

Everyone Makes Mistakes

Have you ever made a mistake on the job?
Chances are that you immediately took steps
to clean up your act. God offers to clean your
slate each day—all you have to do is ask!

Strengths and Weaknesses

Some days my faith is so strong
I can almost see it, Lord. Other
days, my faith seems puny and
weak. Be with me on both my
strong and weak days, because
no matter how I feel, I want to
do Your work. Amen.

For Everyone's Benefit

Thank You, Lord, that life is not a disorganized mess. Thank You, Lord, for teaching us to schedule and to work with each other for the consideration of all.

—PAMELA KAYE TRACY

Day 212

Enriching the Soul

I consider a human soul without education like marble in the quarry, which shows none of its inherent beauties till the skill of the polisher fetches out the colors, makes the surface shine, and discovers every ornamental cloud, spot, and vein that runs through the body of it.

—JOSEPH ADDISON

Helping Hands

Remember, if you ever need a helping hand,
you'll find one at the end of your arm. . . .
As you grow older you will discover that you
have two hands. One for helping yourself,
the other for helping others.

—AUDREY HEPBURN

Never Fear

Instead of allowing fear to rule your life, you need to steadfastly rest in Jesus' love. He who holds the entire world in His hands can direct your life in the face of bad opinions or situations.

Planting Seeds

The work is great, Lord.
Whenever I am tempted to throw
up my hands in defeat, remind
me that I am part of Your Body.
Together we plant the seeds;
You will send the rain and ensure
the harvest. Amen.

Day 216

Lean on God

Whom are you trusting with your soul today? Everyone is trusting something or someone, whether they realize it or not. Take time to search your heart and lean on God, who is forever faithful.

Day
217

Life Investment

Lord, I want to offer sacrifices that please
You. Just as I'm delighted when students obey
me, may I, as Your child, please You by
investing in the lives of others.

—DENISE SHUMWAY

Living in the Moment

The art of life is to live in the present moment and to make that moment as perfect as we can by the realization that we are the instruments and expression of God Himself.

—Emmet Fox

Day
219

Erasing Mistakes

As I erase my chalkboard each
evening, Father, help me erase
the memory of a child's mistakes,
so that each new day I can start
fresh with her. Amen.

Day 220

Knowledge Gained

For the LORD gives wisdom; from His mouth
come knowledge and understanding.
He stores up sound wisdom for the upright;
He is a shield to those who walk in integrity.

—PROVERBS 2:6-7 NASB

Day
221

Taking Time to Learn

Getting things done is not always what is most important. There is value in allowing others to learn, even if the task is not accomplished as quickly, efficiently, or effectively.

—R. D. CLYDE

The Provider

Do you wonder if you are depending too much on your boss to provide for your needs? God is your provider. He knows your needs before you ask. Turn to Him and trust that He will provide for your every need.

You Can Do Anything

You can have anything you want,
if you want it badly enough.
You can be anything you want
to be, do anything you set out to
accomplish, if you hold to that
desire with singleness of purpose.

—ABRAHAM LINCOLN

Childlike

The point is to develop the childlike inclination for play and the childlike desire for recognition and to guide the child over to important fields for society. Such a school demands from the teacher that he be a kind of artist in his province.

—ALBERT EINSTEIN

Day
225

Appreciating Opportunities

Responsibility, commitment, effort—they are so important. Lord, help today's students to appreciate the opportunity afforded to them. And help me, Father, to make my classroom one that inspires learning.

—PAMELA KAYE TRACY

Not What It Seems

Ordinary things are not always what they seem. After all, the ordinary-looking Jesus was the only man to rise from the dead and live in eternity. Today, rejoice that you serve a living God.

Protection

Lord, when I feel frightened and
insecure, hide me in the shelter of
Your love. I trust in You to protect
me. Thank You for being by my
side through every circumstance
of life. Amen.

Day 228

Eternal Investment

Lord Jesus, we want to use eternal materials as we build, as we invest in the lives of our students. May our words and deeds be gold, silver, and precious stones that last. Help us to put aside the wood, hay, and stubble, which will be destroyed.

—DENISE SHUMWAY

Day
229

Understanding
God's Ways

In the midst of hurtful situations, you may
have a hard time understanding God's ways.
You want justice. Pray and ask God to show
you that His ways are perfect.

The Simple Life

To find the universal elements enough; to find the air and the water exhilarating; to be refreshed by a morning walk or an evening saunter. . .to be elated over a bird's nest or a wildflower in spring—these are some of the rewards of the simple life.

—JOHN BURROUGHS

Growth through Warmth

One looks back with appreciation to the brilliant teachers, but with gratitude to those who touched our human feelings. The curriculum is so much necessary material, but warmth is the vital element for the growing plant and for the soul of the child.

—CARL JUNG

**Day
232**

Battles to Be Fought

Everyone has to choose which battles to fight and which to avoid. Instead of relying on your own wits and wisdom, turn to God, who will show you where your efforts will be most effective.

Believing in Others

Dear Lord, help me to never be so busy I fail
to encourage, especially those who silently
cry out for my help and can do great things
if someone believes in them.

—COLLEEN L. REECE AND
ANITA CORRINE DONIHUE

Telling Stories

Thoughts flow in terms of
stories—stories about events,
stories about people,
and stories about intentions
and achievements.
The best teachers are the best
storytellers. We learn in the
form of stories.

—FRANK SMITH

A Different Path

Sometimes a new job doesn't work out. When something like this happens, it's easy to ask, "Where was God in all this?" Don't assume God has abandoned you. He may be taking you on a different path, but He hasn't forgotten about you.

No Mistakes

Lord, I find it amazing that You never make mistakes. You not only know all our names, but how many hairs are on our heads! What comfort that gives me. I thank You, Lord, that You watch out for me.

—PAMELA KAYE TRACY

Day
237

Every Blessing

Thank You, Lord, for every blessing,
both big and small. Help me become more
aware of the ways in which You take care of
me. I'll always be willing to share with others
what You've given to me. Amen.

An Escape

O Lord, sometimes we just need to escape. In the midst of a hectic day, we can hide in You. You are a safe place to which we can always run, even when we cannot leave our classrooms.

—DENISE SHUMWAY

Day
239

To-Do List

Before you leave work in the evening, take time to write a to-do list for the next day. Writing down items while they're fresh in your mind will help you have a better tomorrow.

Day 240

Perseverance

Therefore, since we are surrounded by such a great cloud of witnesses, let us throw off everything that hinders and the sin that so easily entangles, and let us run with perseverance the race marked out for us.

—Hebrews 12:1 niv

**Day
241**

Facing Fear

You gain strength, courage, and confidence
by every experience in which you really stop
to look fear in the face. You must do the thing
that you think you cannot do.

—ELEANOR ROOSEVELT

Awakening Curiosity

The whole art of teaching is only the art of awakening the natural curiosity of young minds for the purpose of satisfying it afterwards; and curiosity itself can be vivid and wholesome only in proportion as the mind is contented and happy.

—ANATOLE FRANCE

Overcoming Difficult Days

Days of drudgery—we all have them. Reconnect with God, follow His commands, and He will help you find a solution for your situation—one that will not leave you feeling bored or useless.

**Day
244**

Focus of the Heart

Lord, when troubles assail me, You give me strength to continue by filling my heart with hope. As I trust in You, Lord, strength fills my entire being. Whether I face hard times or good ones, You are forever the focus of my heart. Amen.

Payback Doesn't Pay

People who strike back at those who hurt them may seem to win in the short run, but eventually they, too, get a payback for their sins. If you've been wronged, leave the situation in God's hands, and He will take care of it.

The Ideal Teacher

Keep me humble, Father, remembering the phrase "and a little child shall lead them." Make me into the kind of teacher every parent wants for his or her child. Amen.

A Nurturing Environment

Feelings of worth can flourish
only in an atmosphere where
individual differences are
appreciated, mistakes are
tolerated, communication is open,
and rules are flexible—the kind
of atmosphere that is found
in a nurturing family.

—Virginia Satir

Day 248

The Path of Lifelong Learning

The great awareness comes slowly, piece by piece. The path of spiritual growth is a path of lifelong learning. The experience of spiritual power is basically a joyful one.

—M. Scott Peck

Day 249

Fear of the Unknown

Are you facing something new—a job or project? Does fear enter your heart at what you're taking on? If it's something God has brought into your life, you can count on Him to see you through.

Opportunities at Work

I thank You, Lord, for my work and the opportunities it brings me. May others not so blessed find the jobs for which they are searching. May we all work in a manner that brings glory to You. Amen.

Seeing Clearly

When you feel like an ant
compared to coworkers,
huge projects, or anything else,
start looking at yourself through
the right lens. Are you seeing
your working life through God's
eyes or your own?

Day 252

Rest Is Not a Waste

Rest is not idleness, and to lie sometimes on the grass on a summer day listening to the murmur of water, or watching the clouds float across the sky, is hardly a waste of time.

—JOHN LUBBOCK

Day
253

A Loving Example

Thank You, Father, for Your help,
support, and provision as I age. May I use
these years to glorify Your name, so that
my life will serve as an example to younger
generations of Your strength and care. Amen.

Encourage Originality

Ideal teachers are those who use themselves as bridges over which they invite their students to cross, then having facilitated their crossing, joyfully collapse, encouraging them to create bridges of their own.

—NIKOS KAZANTZAKIS

Gain Experience along the Way

If you are young, you can do a good job. You may not have experience, but you have a brain and ambition. You can learn what you need to know and address yourself seriously to the work at hand. As you do your part, God will open up new opportunities.

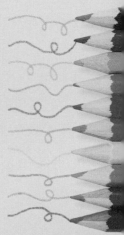

Day 256

Wealth Is Not Worthy

Riches are the least worthy of gifts which God can give a man. What are they to God's Word, to bodily gifts, such as beauty and health, or to the gifts of the mind, such as understanding, skill, wisdom!

—MARTIN LUTHER

Stay Positive

Sometimes as Christians we can be naïve.
The workplace has a way of waking us up to
what others think and feel. Being realistic
is fine, but ask God to guard your heart
so you don't become a cynic.

Nobody's Perfect

Teach me not to expect
perfection from my children.
Help me explain that I am far
from perfect and that I know
they will make mistakes. Let
me show them that I will always
love them, as You love me.
Amen.

Cherish Beauty

Cherish your visions;
cherish your ideals; cherish the
music that stirs in your heart,
the beauty that forms in your
mind, the loveliness that drapes
your purest thoughts, for out
of them will grow all delightful
conditions, all heavenly
environment.

—JAMES ALLEN

Day 260

The Renewing of Your Mind

And do not be conformed to this world, but be transformed by the renewing of your mind, that you may prove what is that good and acceptable and perfect will of God.

—ROMANS 12:2 NKJV

God Our Provider

God is your provider. He is the One who
provides you with your job, your home,
and your daily food. When you face problems on
the job or need money to pay your bills, you can
turn to Him and ask for wisdom and provision.

Day 262

Education Teaches Good Judgment

The supreme end of education is expert discernment in all things—the power to tell the good from the bad, the genuine from the counterfeit, and to prefer the good and the genuine to the bad and the counterfeit.

—SAMUEL JOHNSON

The Best Resource

When you're having a tough workday, are you tapping into your best resource? Do you take a few minutes on break or at lunchtime to connect with your heavenly Father? If so, you're part of the best working team available—and nothing will faze you for long.

Day 264

Hold Your Tongue

Do not let any unwholesome talk come out of your mouths, but only what is helpful for building others up according to their needs, that it may benefit those who listen.

—EPHESIANS 4:29 NIV

Day 265

The Blessings of Children

Thank You, Father, for the blessings of children. Bless their souls. Help them to search for and find You. Let me, as their teacher, reach out to each one. Amen.

Listening to Children

One of God's richest blessings. . .is that our children come into the world as people we're supposed to guide and direct, and then God uses them to form us—if we will only listen.

—DENA DYER

Constructing Eternal Lessons

Lord, we want to be wise, not foolish, builders—in our schools, in our homes, and in our churches. We want our work to be strong enough to withstand the troubles and storms that will come. May we build with eternal materials upon You, our Rock.

—DENISE SHUMWAY

Day 268

Mission Work

Lord, in Your generous, gracious love,
You cared for me even when I ignored You.
Help me to love others as You have loved me.
I want to be part of Your mission to open
blind eyes and raise bowed-down hearts.
Amen.

Day
269

Faithfulness in All Tasks

Noah took on an enormous job when he built
the ark—cutting the wood, shaping it, fitting
it together, and then adding stinky pitch.
He never complained but just obeyed as
onlookers mocked. God wants us to be
faithful no matter what the task.

Compassion

How far you go in life depends on your being tender with the young, compassionate with the aged, sympathetic with the striving, and tolerant of the weak and the strong. Because someday in life you will have been all of those.

—GEORGE WASHINGTON CARVER

**Day
271**

Share the
Prosperity

"At the end of every third year,
bring the entire tithe of that
year's harvest and store it in
the nearest town. . . . Then the
LORD your God will bless you
in all your work."

—DEUTERONOMY 14:28–29 NLT

Day
272

Tackling an
Impossible Project

Do you face an impossible task today?
Perhaps you need to get a huge project done
in a short amount of time. Ask God to help you
with the impossible. All things are possible
with Him.

**Day
273**

A Generous Boss

If your boss has given you sympathy,
support, and encouragement while you
faced challenges at home or in the workplace,
you've been blessed. Take time to share
your gratitude with him or her.

Day 274

Bringing Good to Colleagues

Turn my spirit toward You
again, Lord, where I can find
the joy and contentment I'm
missing. May I feel Your Spirit
touch my heart so that I may
bring good to those I see
each day. Amen.

God's Guidance

Ask God to guide you as you share your faith or take a stand for what is right. He will direct you as you speak and share the truth.

Day 276

Someone Your Students Can Trust

Help me to be a support to my students who may have no support at home. I cannot be a parent to them, but make me someone whom they can trust. Amen.

Day
277

Reminder of the Future

When you do sin, and you will from time
to time, God does not condemn you and
leave you to your own way. He draws you
to Him with His love and reminds you
of your future with Him.

A Powerful Testimony

Dear Father, may I always be aware that others are watching me, looking for evidence of Your presence in my life. As Your Word guides and strengthens me, may the good works You lead me to do be a powerful testimony to my coworkers and students.

—DENISE SHUMWAY

No Matter the Circumstances

You never can measure what God will do through you. . . . Keep your relationship right with Him; then whatever circumstances you are in, and whoever you meet day by day, He is pouring rivers of living water through you.

—OSWALD CHAMBERS

Day 280

Every Word Counts

"I tell you the truth, until heaven and earth disappear, not the smallest letter, not the least stroke of a pen, will by any means disappear from the Law until everything is accomplished."

—MATTHEW 5:18 NIV

Dealing with Problem Students

Lord, give me wisdom to deal with the problem students, especially the tardy students and the often truant students. Help me to find a way to keep them on track. Amen.

Never-Changing Love

In the Bible, Paul tells us that he considered everything a loss compared to knowing Jesus. You may go through a job loss or the loss of a loved one, but you still have the never-changing love of Jesus Christ—the same yesterday, today, and forever.

Day
283

Failure Is the Teacher's Failure

Don't try to fix the students;
fix ourselves first. The good
teacher makes the poor student
good and the good student
superior. When our students fail,
we, as teachers, too, have failed.

—Marva Collins

Sources of Support

When troubles come, to whom do you go?
Getting some support from others is a
good thing—at home, on the job, and in the
community. Don't forget to call out to God for
help as well. He is only a prayer away.

A Lifetime of
Experience Shared

A long lifetime of experience brings wisdom
that should be shared. Keep my heart young
and my spirit strong, Father, so I may do
Your work throughout my life. Amen.

A Well-Functioning School

Father, how wonderfully You made our bodies, and what a picture they are of coordination. We long for our schools to function in the same way, with each member performing a different job, working together with all the other members for the good of the whole.

—Denise Shumway

Carefully Chosen Words

God says that people who make
peace will be blessed. Before you
approach a tough situation at
work, ask God for discernment.
Really listen to what the other
person has to say and choose
your words carefully.

Day 288

The Genius of Each Child

Do not train children in learning by force
and harshness, but direct them to it by
what amuses their minds, so that you may
be better able to discover with accuracy the
peculiar bent of the genius of each.

—Plato

Day
289

Ask Questions and Inspire Questions

The test of a good teacher is not how many questions he can ask his pupils that they will answer readily, but how many questions he inspires them to ask him which he finds it hard to answer.

—ALICE WELLINGTON ROLLINS

The Road Rightfully Taken

Father, I want my life to count. I know in Your eyes it already does—always has. Guide my decisions and direct my paths in ways that best suit Your purposes. Please use me as only You can. Amen.

Not Forgotten

When trouble hits your
workplace, it is easy to wonder
who is in change. God hasn't
forgotten you, your family, or
your coworkers. When God has
you in His hand, He's in control of
your life—no matter what happens
in the rest of the world.

Day 292

Mornings Bring New Opportunity

Mornings glitter with the potential for opportunity. Lord, remind me to embrace each morning and to greet my students as if this will be the best day of their lives— every day.

—PAMELA KAYE TRACY

Day
293

Seeing as a Child Sees

In order to manage children well,
we must borrow their eyes and their hearts,
see and feel as they do, and judge them
from their own point of view.

—Eugénie de Guérin

Teaching with Grace

As teachers, we recognize that
our ability is a gift from You,
and we want to use it to bring
glory to You. We want to teach
according to the grace You give.
We desire to be Your hands,
reaching out to others, and Your
mouth, speaking truth and life.

—DENISE SHUMWAY

When Work Is Overwhelming

Have you ever been so overwhelmed with work that you felt you had to quit because there was no way out? Instead of making a rash decision, speak with your supervisor and express your feelings. Many times help is available if you just ask.

Day 296

Perfect Timing

Teach me patience as I wait—the patience that comes from putting my confidence in You and Your perfect timing. When my frustration begins to build, remind me of Your sovereignty and goodness. Thank You, Lord.

Day
297

Different Words for Different Situations

Lord, I thank You for giving me words to both teach my students and communicate with my [family]. Help me to always take care when choosing my words.

—PAMELA KAYE TRACY

Day 298

Not a Minute Wasted

Tomorrow is a new day; begin it well and serenely and with too high a spirit to be cumbered with your old nonsense. This day is all that is good and fair. It is too dear, with its hopes and invitations, to waste a moment on yesterdays.

—RALPH WALDO EMERSON

Praying through the Day

Father, it seems I don't have time
to stop and kneel to pray.
Teach me to weave a pattern of
ongoing prayer into the fabric of
my teaching day. Amen.

Day 300

A New Thing

"Do not remember the former things, nor consider the things of old. Behold, I will do a new thing, now it shall spring forth; shall you not know it? I will even make a road in the wilderness and rivers in the desert."

—Isaiah 43:18–19 NKJV

Inspiring Students' Natural Abilities

The good teacher. . .discovers the natural gifts of his pupils and liberates them by the stimulating influence of the inspiration that he can impart. The true leader makes his followers twice the men they were before.

—STEPHEN NEILL

The Meagerness of Money

The Bible says the love of money is the root of all evil. God knows you need money to live, but it's your attitude toward money with which He is concerned. He wants you to trust in Him, not money, to supply all your needs.

Day
303

Serving Together

Thank You, Father, for all those
who serve by their work as staff,
janitors, cafeteria workers,
bus drivers, office workers,
and maintenance workers. Bless
them every one, Lord. Amen.

Day 304

In the Spirit of Love

You will find as you look back upon your life that the moments when you have really lived are the moments when you have done things in the spirit of love.

—HENRY DRUMMOND

**Day
305**

Your Specific Assignment

Thank You, Lord, for the school system You
have placed me in—for the specific students
You have placed in my classroom. May I be
worthy of my assignment. Amen.

Focus on Things Above

Lord, how often I act as if my life was all about the details of my schedule. The truth is that my life is in You. Today, Father, I want to focus on the "things above."

—DENISE SHUMWAY

Something New

Often, old tried and true ways are best—but not always. At times the old ways need to give way to the new. God can make you fresh by giving you new life in Jesus. Ask Him to make your life new, and He will.

Day 308

Each Person's Contribution

Many in this world might consider themselves "nobodies"—the poor, the oppressed, the hardworking. But they are made beautiful by their meek and quiet spirits. Thank You, Lord, for showing me that every person is a source of joy for You. Amen.

Individual Personalities

The most important function of
education at any level is to develop the
personality of the individual and the
significance of his life to himself and to others.
This is the basic architecture of a life;
the rest is ornamentation and decoration
of the structure.

—GRAYSON KIRK

Small Acts of Kindness

Too often we underestimate the power of a touch, a smile, a kind word, a listening ear, an honest compliment, or the smallest act of caring, all of which have the potential to turn a life around.

—Leo Buscaglia

Gloominess, Be Gone

When any fit of anxiety or gloominess or perversion of the mind lays hold upon you, make it a rule not to publish it by complaints but exert your whole care to hide it. By endeavoring to hide it, you will drive it away.

—SAMUEL JOHNSON

Day 312

Questions and Decisions

God has promised to give you wisdom when you ask. Today as you face questions and decisions, call on Him for wisdom. He'll be pleased to give it to you so you can benefit others.

A Little Prod

Teachers: two kinds: the kind that fill you
with so much quail shot that you can't move
and the kind that just give you a little prod
from behind and you jump to the skies.

—ROBERT FROST

Keep On Keeping On

Some days it's tough to press on. Work isn't exciting. You wonder why you do what you do and where it will lead you. Stop and remind yourself of God's promises to those who are diligent.

The Gift of Giving

Lord Jesus, not everyone has
the gift of giving, but in this
profession, we all need to be
givers. We are called upon to give
time, energy, care, and support.

—DENISE SHUMWAY

Day 316

A Cheery Attitude

Lord, help me to keep such a cheerful outlook on life that it shows in my countenance. Make me a ray of sunshine to students who are starved for light. Amen.

Day 317

True Potential

Lord, I want to reach my true potential and become the person You created me to be. Show me how I can best put my unique gifts, circumstances, and relationship with You to use in ways that will make a positive difference in this world. Amen.

Never Give Up

Never let your head hang down.
Never give up and sit down and
grieve. Find another way.
And don't pray when it rains if you
don't pray when the sun shines.

—SATCHEL PAIGE

Celebrating Today's Joys

Lord, remind me to celebrate every moment in my classroom and cherish each day. Let me not worry about tomorrow so much that I miss out on the joys of today. Amen.

**Day
320**

The Shelter of Wisdom

Wisdom, like an inheritance, is a good thing and benefits those who see the sun. Wisdom is a shelter as money is a shelter, but the advantage of knowledge is this: that wisdom preserves the life of its possessor.

—ECCLESIASTES 7:11–12 NIV

Day 321

Prayer Anywhere

Pray wherever you are—on the way to work, during lunch hour, before meals, or while you're doing your least favorite household chore. Any time is a good time to pray.

Needing Encouragement

Dear Lord, I'm constantly amazed at how You bring encouragement into my life at just the right time, just when I need it most. Thank You for bringing other people into my life to show me Your love. Amen.

Teaching Is Important

If kids come to us from strong, healthy, functioning families, it makes our job easier. If they do not come to us from strong, healthy, functioning families, it makes our job more important.

—BARBARA COLOROSO

Day 324

The Right Attitude

Lord, thank You for promising to supply my needs when I bring them to You. I pray for the right attitude to teach with the equipment and materials I have. Amen.

Day
325

Shared Happiness

Happiness is a sunbeam. . . . When it
strikes a kindred heart, like the converged
lights upon a mirror, it reflects itself
with redoubled brightness. It is not
perfected until it is shared.

—JANE PORTER

God Is in Charge

Although there are many wise, mighty, and rich people in the world, never forget that the God you serve is in charge. It is your job to bring glory to Him, and He will watch over the details of your life.

Using the Correct Words

Lord, saying the correct words to get the same message across to different types of parents is a skill in itself. I ask for courage to speak the truth and for a receiving heart to hear the truth.

—Pamela Kaye Tracy

Day 328

Stay Organized!

Take time to keep records in good order. Good documentation and organized files can save you hours of time on future projects, preventing you from having to invent the wheel for each new project.

Doing What You Don't Want To

Perhaps the most valuable result of all
education is the ability to make yourself do
the thing you have to do, when it ought to be
done, whether you like it or not.

—THOMAS HUXLEY

Finding Success In Your Students' Success

What nobler profession than to touch the next generation— to see children hold your understanding in their eyes, your hope in their lives, your world in their hands. In their success you find your own, and so to them you give your all.

—Unknown

Open Doors

Father, I want to have open
doors for everyone You bring
my way. May the doors of my
classroom—and of my heart—be
open to friends and strangers
alike. May no one ever feel lonely
or burdened because my door
was closed to them.

—DENISE SHUMWAY

Turning Points

When you come to a happy turning point in your life, do you rush to thank God? Or do you assume that your own abilities have brought you to where you are? Take time to praise God for the blessings He has poured out upon you.

Day
333

A Nudge in the
Right Direction

Father, nudge me when I grow bored and
sloppy at work. I don't want to be the kind of
worker who cuts corners and gives less and
less. I want to be known as a diligent worker.
Thank You for keeping me on track. Amen.

The True Art of Questioning

Most teachers waste their time by asking questions which are intended to discover what a pupil does not know, whereas the true art of questioning has for its purpose to discover what the pupil knows or is capable of knowing.

—ALBERT EINSTEIN

Useful Education

Father, bless me with a vision to
see the lasting results of my work.
Give me a vision of the students
grown and using their education
in their homes and workplaces.
Amen.

Day 336

Open Eyes

Half the joy of life is in little things taken on the run. Let us run if we must. . .but let us keep our hearts young and our eyes open that nothing worth our while shall escape us. And everything is worth its while if we only grasp it and its significance.

—CHARLES VICTOR CHERBULIEZ

Day
337

Facing Opposition

No matter who you are or what you do,
at times people will threaten or discourage
you. You may not triumph over every
bit of opposition, but follow God and
He will see that you prosper.

The Right Way

I know You want the best for
me, Lord, and You will provide
it. My job is to live my life
in a way that glorifies You.
Everything beyond that is a
blessing. I choose to be content.
Amen.

You Are What You Are

By the grace of God I am what
I am, and His grace toward me
was not in vain; but I labored
more abundantly than they all,
yet not I, but the grace of God
which was with me.

—1 CORINTHIANS 15:10 NKJV

Day 340

Appropriate Behavior

The soldiers likewise demanded of him, saying, And what shall we do? And he said unto them, Do violence to no man, neither accuse any falsely; and be content with your wages.

—LUKE 3:14 KJV

Day
341

The Game of Life

Whether sixty or sixteen, there is in every human being's heart the love of wonder, the sweet amazement at the stars and starlike things, the undaunted challenge of events, the unfailing childlike appetite for what-next, and the joy of the game of living.

—SAMUEL ULLMAN

Constant Guidance

In our world, change is constant. Jobs, homes, and technology can all be challenging to keep up with. However, Jesus is the same yesterday, today, and forever. He will be your guide and rock.

Classroom Rules

In our classrooms, we either
reward or discipline our students
for their behavior. May we always
use Your Word as the basis of
our rules, even if we can't teach
the scripture directly. Grant us
wisdom, Lord, in dealing with our
students, as well as our society
as a whole.

—DENISE SHUMWAY

**Day
344**

Cherish Demanding Days

Let me cherish busy days with young people,
happy to have a part in their world. Help
me to learn to slow down and relax in my
teaching. Amen.

Day
345

Self-Sufficiency

In the final analysis, it is not what you do for
your children but what you have taught them
to do for themselves that will make them
successful human beings.

—Ann Landers

Moving Forward

When I'm feeling weak and
vulnerable, Lord, You are the
only One I can turn to for help.
Strengthen me; energize me.
Fill me with Your power and
might, that I may move forward
to accomplish those things that
You've placed on my heart.
Amen.

Dear Friends

Have you worked with some wonderful people who had to move? No doubt you miss those friends. Take a moment to ask the Lord to watch over them and bless them.

**Day
348**

Rediscovering the World

If a child is to keep alive his inborn sense of wonder, he needs the companionship of at least one adult who can share it, rediscovering with him the joy, the excitement, and the mystery of the world we live in.

—RACHEL CARLSON

Day
349

Life Laws

Thank You for sharing Your wisdom with me,
Lord. You often let me realize the wisdom in
Your rules and plans. I begin to see the design
You have for ruling the world. Rule my life,
also. Your judgments are always wise. Amen.

Teacher Appreciation

Lord, Your followers taught in villages, tiny homes, chariots, and standing on rocks. I have electricity and overheads, and still I expect more. Help me to appreciate all I have.

—PAMELA KAYE TRACY

Asking for Forgiveness

Instead of beating yourself up for any wrong—large or small—do what God asks: Repent and ask His forgiveness. His peace is more important than anything the world has to offer.

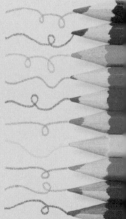

Day
352

Simple Things

Dear Jesus, help me not to be so busy that
I miss the small pleasures You've sprinkled
throughout my day. . . . Give me a child's heart
that sees the lovely, simple things in life.

—ELLYN SANNA

Charity

Remind me, Lord, that though the little I can give seems useless, when added to the little that millions give, my charity can make a difference. Help me to give in faith. Amen.

Take Your Time

Lord, I need resolve to be patient with students in the midst of the ever-increasing demands on my time. Teach me to give students the time they need to absorb information and develop as scholars. Amen.

Paying Attention

What does it take for your boss
to get your attention?
What does it take for God to get
your attention? Sometimes it's
easier to hear an earthly voice
than that heavenly one that calls
you to obedience.

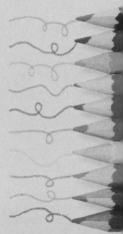

Day 356

Great Men and Women

I studied the lives of great men and famous women, and I found that the men and women who got to the top were those who did the jobs they had in hand, with everything they had of energy and enthusiasm.

—HENRY TRUMAN

Gossip

Scripture says a lot about gossip—
none of it is good. God takes it seriously
and never hands out exceptions for those
things that you "just have to" pass on.
If others gossip to you, defuse the situation
by speaking words of encouragement.

A Fresh Start

You know my heart, Lord.
You know how much I long to be
the person You created me to
be. Please make me new again.
Give me a fresh start. Cover
me once again with Your
forgiveness. Amen.

Day
359

A Secure Classroom

As I grow older, Lord, I need
Your presence around me like a
favorite comforter. It gives me
warmth and security to know that
You are with me as I work in
the classroom. Amen.

Day 360

Seasoned with Salt

Be wise in the way you act toward outsiders; make the most of every opportunity. Let your conversation be always full of grace, seasoned with salt, so that you may know how to answer everyone.

—COLOSSIANS 4:5-6 NIV

Clear Vision

Lord, we would surely perish if we didn't have the vision of Your plan for our lives as teachers. You brought us to this position, You supply us for our duties each day, and You will accomplish Your desire through us wherever we work.

—DENISE SHUMWAY

Refreshment

With work all week and
chores all weekend, rest can
be elusive. Drawing close to God
in prayer—even if it's just for
a few minutes—can rest
and refresh you.

A Sense of Purpose

Help me to persevere to the end, Lord, not with a sense of drudgery and duty but with an energizing fire of joy and purpose, content to trust You for everything I need to succeed. Amen.

Day 364

Job Requirements

Dear God, help me to remember that it is not my job to remake a student, but rather to make him a student by awaking in him the longing to learn. Amen.

**Day
365**

One Is Enough

I am only one, but I am one. I cannot do everything, but I can do something. And that which I can do, by the grace of God, I will do.

—DWIGHT L. MOODY

Notes

Notes

Notes

Notes

Notes

_____

_____

_____

_____

_____

_____

_____

_____

_____

_____

_____

Notes

Notes

_____

_____

_____

_____

_____

_____

_____

_____

_____

_____

_____

Notes

Notes

Notes

_____

_____

_____

_____

_____

_____

_____

_____

_____

_____

_____

Notes

Notes

_____

_____

_____

_____

_____

_____

_____

_____

_____

_____

Notes

Notes

Notes